High Voltage Branding

Go from Ordinary To Extra-Ordinary

By Mitche Graf

Dedication

This book is dedicated to my wonderful wife, Tami, who always puts up with me during times when I'm trying to finish up a book manuscript.

Early mornings in my recliner before the rest of the world is up with a good cup of coffee, my dogs at my feet and a computer on my lap.

So, for all your patience and extra duty that you put in so I can get my "quiet time" I say thank you and

I LOVE YOU!

High Voltage Branding

Go From Ordinary To Extra-Ordinary

© 2020 Mitche Graf

Cover Design: Ryan Lause

Back Cover Photo: Tami Graf

Publisher: Power Marketing 101

P.O. Box 405

Aurora, Oregon 97002 USA

FOR BULK ORDERS OR GROUP DISCOUNTS CALL:

888.719.4692

www.MitcheGraf.com

ISBN: 978-1-7320344-2-6

The 4X Formula-
Getting Twice As Much Done In ½ The Time
(limited spots available)

This course will be launching within the next few weeks, and now you have the opportunity to be part of the inaugural beta "A-Team", who will get some special bonuses that are available only for this group.

BONUS #1-

You'll be given lifetime access to all of the content, including any updates or additions that are made in the future.

BONUS #2-

You also will be given access to a private Facebook group where other students in the course can go to share your struggles, share your wins, and get access to Mitche to discuss the course as it develops.

BONUS #3-

You will also have exclusive access to a monthly live group video call where Mitche answers your questions, helps you with any challenges you are having, and helps facilitate the communications between group members.

And as a special bonus...

BONUS #4-

We will also send you a digital copy of the book "The Unleashed Entrepreneur – A Kick-Ass Guide To Harnessing Your Inner Ninja, Working Less, & Designing Your Perfect Lifestyle" as my gift to you.

The bonuses alone are valued at over $500, and the course will be selling for $250 once we launch this to the rest of the world.

That's A Total Value Of Over $750!

But you don't need to pay anywhere near that.

Right now, you can grab the course and the other bonuses for only $100, or 2 payments of $60 each.

ENROLL NOW
at
www.4xcourse.com

A SPECIAL THANK YOU NOTE

I deeply appreciate you taking the time to invest in your quality of life, your business, and your future! If you find the book to be beneficial, I would be grateful if you would leave an honest review on Amazon. It would mean the world to me!

Looking for more inspiration and actionable tools to grow your business and design your perfect lifestyle? Then subscribe to the hottest new show the "Business Edge Radio" with Mitche Graf on iTunes, Stitcher, Google Play, Spotify, or on your local talk radio station. Hear dynamic interviews with world-class entrepreneurs as well as regular dose of meat-and-potatoes techniques that will ignite your superpowers to achieve even greater things!

Additional resources can be found at www.MitcheGraf.com.

Thank you for spending this time with me, and good luck with your new set of eyes!

Mitche

Table of Contents

About Your Captain.. *i*

INTRODUCTION.. *v*

Chapter 1: Image is Everything 1

Chapter 2: 5-Second Image Challenge............................ 15

Chapter 3: Perception is Everything 35

Chapter 4: Real vs. Perceived Value 49

Chapter 5: Personal Branding 59

Chapter 6: Developing a "Blue Ocean" Strategy 69

Chapter 7: Delivering a "6-Star Experience"................... 77

Chapter 8: How To Build A Cult Brand 83

Chapter 9: Is My Brand Broke? 93

About Your Captain

Best-selling author, serial entrepreneur, inter-national-renowned business speaker, former All-American Track & Field athlete, and Daddy-of-Three Mitche Graf has been a passionate serial entrepreneur for over 30 years, dangling his toes into the ponds of many intriguing industries along the way.

From selling used bicycle parts out of his garage in the seventh grade to running three companies today, he has prided himself on knowing how to squeeze every drop of potential out of his endeavors.

Over the past three decades, Mitche has created two award-winning restaurants, a bustling internationally-known catering & events company, a national spice manufacturing business with over 4000 accounts, a photography studio, a cribbage board manufacturing company, an award-winning limousine business, a portable hot tub rental business, a drive-through espresso company, an educational products company, an athletic fitness testing corporation, and even a nightcrawler company.

In the middle of all this, he also was given the once-in-a-lifetime opportunity to become the President of Business Operations for an affiliate of the world champion San Francisco Giants baseball team, increasing attendance by 12% which was one of the biggest in all professional baseball.

Having started, built, and successfully operated numerous enterprises in a multitude of industries has taught him a simple truth: the same basic business principles apply, regardless of the arena you may play in.

As an educator and motivational speaker, Mitche's high-voltage seminars and workshops have been delivered around the world to over 75,000 people in 9 countries and nearly every state in the U.S., and his techniques have resulted in over $1,000,000,000 in sales from his innovative ideas. His cutting-edge articles and columns have appeared in the pages of business trade magazines such as Rangefinder, PPA Magazine, Limo Digest, Chauffer Driven, Image Maker, and Fresh Cup Magazine, as well as many online marketing sites and blogs.

He is passionate about the outdoors and laughing, playing guitar, reading, listening to great music, cooking and eating, drinking good wine, taking a tremendous amount of time off to chill, and most importantly, spending time with his family.

Mitche lives in a small country town in Oregon with his wife Tami and their three small children Jaycee, Colton, and Sierra, Tilly & Delilah the Dogs, Coral the Hermit Crab as well several hundred guppies (names not important).

He spends much of his time looking for ways to work smarter, not harder, so he can spend more time doing and enjoying the things in life that are most important to him.

He believes that EVERY DAY IS A SATURDAY, and this perspective inspires him to wake up every day with a sense of excitement and enthusiasm to live his life by design.

INTRODUCTION

In my 30-plus years of starting and building businesses, I can honestly say that I have had more fun branding each one of them than anything else. Designing the look and feel of the graphics, determining who my perfect customers will be, deciding on how to create perceived value-adds in the minds of those perfect customers, and of course launching each brand to the world to consume.

Whether it has been a service business, a digital products business, a manufacturing company or a combination, my endorphins get pumping and my creative juices flowing when I begin to develop a brand.

The joy I get when I see one of my concepts take hold in the marketplace is gratifying beyond explanation and keeps me up at night with excitement. It's what keeps my mind constantly cranking out innovative and cutting-edge ideas at breakneck speeds. Once I begin standing still, my competition will pass me in the blink of an eye, so I am constantly challenging myself to stay one step ahead.

Show me a successful company and at the forefront of their efforts will be an impeccable and well-designed brand that has been painstakingly create along the way. A brand is the lifeblood of any business and can make the difference between success and failure. In today's cut-throat business environment, the traditional "branding" that you need to get the competitive edge is different from the old days before the Internet.

A strong case can be made that having a top-shelf brand today is more important than it ever has been. The chaotic world of the Internet has taken over what seems to be every aspect of business operation and with it the loss of traditional branding.

Today, you must have a "high voltage" brand that excites prospects and customers in ways never imagined back even just a few years ago. Your business card, website, the way you dress, your marketing collateral, the content you create, the way you answer your phone......all must be broken down and rebuilt with a new perspective and sharper focus.

High Voltage Branding is the simple process of super-charging your efforts so that you leave your competition in your wake and separate yourself from the rest of the pack. And it's not something that you do one time then congratulate yourself on a job well done. Good branding must be part of your mindset each second of each hour of each day of your business life.

"Old brands must be made new, and new brands must be built to feel old. It's a symphony of challenges that can drive you to heights never images before or can cause you to become a huddled mass in the corner."

My challenge to you is this.........I task you to approach this book with an open mind, a willing spirit, and a desire to change for the better.

This change will require a monumental mindset shift that starts in the heart & soul of every business owner and spreads like wildfire throughout the business world.

Today, that mindset shift begins with you and by the end of this read my hope for you is that you will have a "new set of eyes" for what your brand is today and what it can become tomorrow.

Are you ready to get started?

Chapter 1:

Image is Everything

I want to take you on a journey to a place where everything is perfect, where there is no stress or worry, and the streets are made of cheese. It's a place where you can buy anything, do anything, and be anything you want to be. This place is called your mind, and it is the most powerful tool we have been given.

Imagine it's a beautiful, warm Saturday afternoon in the fall, and you decide to go for a drive in the country. With all the hustle and bustle of everyday life, you don't get this opportunity as much as you would like, but today is your day. As you drive along, you decide to head over to a nearby lake that is known for its vibrant fall colors, and tranquil silence. Along the way, you notice that the leaves on the trees next to the road and on the hillside are slowly beginning to softly fall to the ground, as they create a bed of color on the pavement in front of you. With the window down, you can feel the wind tickling your face and you can smell the mustiness of fall. The sun is directly in front of you, and as the sun hits your face, you feel the warmth of its touch.

It's a feeling you crave and relish, and you want to soak up as much of this feeling as possible before the season passes, and winter digs in. You come to the road that will take you to the lake, and you take notice of the fact there are no other cars on the road coming or going……. The road is yours. You begin to feel the excitement of being at the lake by yourself and soaking up all it has to offer.

As you approach the lake, you find a place to park your car, and you begin the short walk down to the lake. You are about 100 yards or so from the bank, and you notice two little stores next to the road… one on the left, and one on the right. Your eyes first are attracted to the rustic-looking brown building on the right. You notice the broken rain gutter that is filled with moldy leaves from last season, and the grass hasn't been cut for quite some time.

There is a bike lying on its side in front, and you can tell it has seen better days…. The handlebars are covered with rust, and several of the spokes are missing from the rear tire. The dark brown paint that is around the windows and door is beginning to chip from age, and there are a couple of spiders that have made their home in the upper corner. The sign above the door reads…. Lakeside QuikMart. The smaller sign in the window above the spider web reads: Lemonade .50 cents and cookies - 10 for a dollar.

Your eyes then meander to the little white building on the other side of the road. There are bright red geraniums neatly planted in oak barrels that are placed along a cobblestone walkway leading up to the front entrance. The white picket fence the surrounds the entire building has tulips all around, and a Post Office box in the shape of a Trout sits atop a cast iron stake. On top of the building, a freshly painted sign reads "Heaven on Earth Country Store" with beautiful blues and greens and yellow throughout…. And then on a smaller sign below, the words, "Where Friends Meet." It almost makes you feel like you are at Grandma's house when you were little…safe, kind, and friendly.

You notice a small sign in the window that says, "Hand-squeezed Country Style lemonade made fresh this morning… only $2.00 a glass. Your mouth begins to water as you imagine drinking that glass of hand-squeezed Country Style fresh lemonade. The side windows are cracked open just enough that you can smell the fresh chocolate chip cookies that must have just pulled out of the oven only 10 seconds before. You would pay just about anything to have a bite of one of those cookies right now.

You pause for a moment, and glance at the brown building on the right side of the road, and then you glance back to the white building on the left side... You must make a choice of which place to go. Hmmm...Your mind is made up. You are going to _____.

Was there really any doubt as to which business you were going to go into? I don't think so. It didn't matter that the price was more, did it? It came down to the image that each business created in your mind.... And once that impression is made, it's virtually impossible to change how we feel.

The QuikMart may have had the best cookies in the world, but they sure didn't create much desire on our part to give them a try, for any price. The same process happens with your business. Judgments are made about you long before you speak the first words to a prospect.

I have always viewed branding as the cornerstone of all my businesses, regardless of the industry they are in. It's one of those things that you either absolutely are in love with or view it as a necessary evil in your business.

Regardless of your opinion, there is 1 absolute fact...

"Your BRAND will determine if you are around in 1 year, 5 years, or 10 years from now."

Crush it and your odds are exponentially increased. Drop the ball and you will be a corpse on the side of the business highway.

Did you know that we as human beings make judgments of people, businesses, food, and other products within 5 seconds? 5 seconds. That sure doesn't give us much time before a decision has been made about how a potential customer feels about us, and what kind of value they believe us to have. You must always be prepared to be judged.

Marketing, positioning, and image creation are much more than Facebook ads and direct mail pieces. It's the expression of who you are and what you do. It's all about what you wear, how you look, the way you walk and talk, the way you communicate with the rest of the world. It's as much about essence, as it is substance.

Most of us have been working our entire career trying to figure out the magic of branding and marketing and are met with great amounts of frustration. We become PhD's from the School of Hard Knocks. We are constantly trying to reinvent the wheel instead of looking outside the box for the answers. Usually there is a simple answer for most obstacles.

Man's discovery of fire was huge, but it took us over 1 million years for us to figure out how to utilize it. Did you know ice cream was invented over 2000 years BC… but it wasn't until only 100 years ago someone came up with the idea for the ice cream cone. In 1775, the flush toilet and in 1857, 82 years later, toilet paper arrived!

We are surrounded with simple solutions to help us succeed. We just don't always see them. And some of the simplest things we normally don't even think about are right in front of our nose, yet we can't see the forest through the trees. Creating a positive image is done in much the same way. The things that make the biggest difference are the littlest of things.

Having a positive image will not only assure your survival in difficult times, it will also allow you to outshine your competition and prosper, even in tough times, because you will be one of the only people in your market place who markets smart. PT Barnum used to say he knew that half of all the money he spent on advertising was wasted if you could just figure out which half....

You can avoid costly mistakes by learning from other people's mistakes or from borrowing valuable lessons from other industries. There is nothing wrong with that. You should study the leaders in your industry and in others and see what it is that gives them the competitive edge. When you do things the same old way, you should expect the same old results. If you hit your head up against a wall and it gives you a headache... STOP DOING IT! You need to spend time observing and studying the most successful and innovative people. We will take you step by step through this process with the 5-second Image Challenge a little bit later.

As businesspeople and entrepreneurs, we make mistakes every day, but the most successful people in any industry are the ones who learn quickly from those mistakes and make the necessary changes to prevent those mistakes from happening again.

"They fail fast and move on."

When it comes down to our branding efforts, most of our mistakes fall within 4 areas:

1) **Failure to Have a Well Thought Out Marketing Plan -** Anyone can captain the ship when the seas are calm. However, a good marketing plan does its best work when the seas are anything BUT calm. 80% of all businesses do not have any form of marketing plan at all... and 80% of all businesses aren't around in 5 years. Do you think this is just a coincidence? We have 2 jobs: 1 - to manage our customers and 2 – to market. Everything else is secondary.

2) **Failure to Have A Clearly Defined Hook or Message -** Without it, you are just a me too, an also ran, another run-of-the-mill business. You will not become successful simply because you are the best. Da Vinci was dead for over 200 years before he became famous. I don't know about you, but I don't want to wait that long!

You need to know what it is that makes you special and unique in your marketplace. What is it that customers can't get from anyone else but you? What is your compelling reason that customers should come to your business instead of all others in your industry? Again, the numbers speak for themselves - 80% of all businesses couldn't tell you what their hook is, if asked. Are you one of the 80%, or do you want to be part of the 20% who make a difference?

3) **Failure to Have Professional-Looking Marketing Pieces -** It's all about first impressions. Everything you do must match your image. If you want to be known for BMW quality, then everything you do should be consistent with that goal.

4) **Failure to Project Your Sales and Goals into the Future -** Let me ask you a question…. Do you already have your personal and professional goals put in writing for the next 12 months? What about for the next 6 months, or 3 months? If it is your goal, and I don't mean just something you talk about but never do, I mean a true-blue goal…. to take at least 2 week-long vacations with your family in the next 12 months, you will need to incorporate that into your business plan in the coming months, right?

You will need to schedule the time off in your calendar book, allocated additional money for your "Vacation Fund" each month, and of course make the appropriate plans to have your business continue to operate in your absence. But the problem with most business owners is that they allow the business to dictate whether they will have the time, or the financial resources to make it happen. They have the excuse of "well, things have been slow lately, and I can't really afford to take any time off for a vacation.

Again, if it's important enough to you, you will figure out a way to make it happen. If you really want it to happen, and you take the necessary steps to accomplish it, it will happen - guaranteed. If you want to increase your gross income for the remainder of the year, you had better start making those plans and projections today. You need to price your products and services to allow for costs, overhead, and that 4-letter word – Profit!

With 4 out of 5 businesses being out of business in less than 5 years, making sure you have a thorough understanding of your cost breakdown on your products, and how much profit is generated from each sale is vital. How many of your products will you need to sell, or what number of service calls will you need to perform to achieve your financial and personal goals? What do you want to make this year, and next year, and the year after that?

The biggest problem in most industries isn't that businesses are priced to cheaply, it's that we they are afraid to charge what they are worth.

If you would like to eliminate a certain segment of the business you currently do, **then start making a game plan today**. Figure out how you can smoothly exit that market and replace it with sales from your more lucrative types of customers. To truly focus, you must do LESS. You can practice hand grenade marketing…. Throw a bunch of stuff out there and hope it hits the target…. Or you can use laser beam marketing and hit only what you want.

The old saying**….**

"If you want to attract a 99 cent customer, get one 99 cent customer because if they like you, they will tell all their other 99 cent friends, which means you will have a bunch of 99 cent customers."

If you do a professional job and remember the value and power of the all mighty referral, they come to you already sold.

They understand your quality, your process, and your pricing. If a customer comes to you and says, *"My neighbor showed me their whatsahoosit, and I absolutely love it, and I want to get one for myself…and oh yea… they said they only spent 99 cents…. I can't wait."* Your pricing strategy is an integral part of your brand, so it's something to be aware of.

It is just like the Lakeside QuikMart store example. It's going to take an awful lot of convincing to get us to spend even .50 cents on a glass of lemonade, or a buck on 5 cookies... Now, there is profit in the 99 cent customer, but you need to sell to a lot more of them than you do the $100, $1000, or $10,000 customer.

"It all comes down to what are your goals in life. Sometimes you are better off going fishing then taking a job that doesn't help you achieve your ultimate objectives and goals."

It's difficult to turn down business at first, but in the long run it will be healthier for your business and yourself. Let's face it...some customers are just not worth having. You have the ultimate say in how you spend your time.

Do you remember when it was you started disliking snakes, or spiders, or flying, or seafood, or asparagus? You may not remember a specific incident, but I bet you are acutely aware of the things in life you do and don't like. Most of those precepts, or beliefs, were embedded deep in our psyche from experiences that lasted 5, 10, maybe 15 seconds. Those precepts have been branded into your brain, which is where the term comes from.

When I was younger, I didn't like asparagus and couldn't tell you why or what it tasted like. I just knew I didn't like it. When I became an adult, I had the opportunity to have some with a meal, and didn't want to be rude, so I scooped up a serving...... and believe it or not, I liked it! I couldn't remember the time I decided asparagus was to be put on my list of things I didn't care for, but my subconscious mind had made up its mind. I'm sure you can think of several things in life you don't like, but can you remember when your dislike began?

The same dynamic happens when we are exposed to people and businesses. That very first impression infiltrates our mind and a judgment is made very quickly. In business, those judgments can either mean future success, or ultimate failure.

Chapter 2:

5-Second Image Challenge

Now, we are going to dive into what I call the 5-Second Image Challenge. As human beings and consumers, we make mental judgments in our minds daily. Right or wrong, within 5 seconds of seeing, feeling, hearing, smelling, or tasting something. We decide in our subconscious minds whether we like something. Those judgments can stay with us our entire lives in many cases.

We are going to be taking a close look at every aspect of what your business looks like, sounds like, and feels like to a potential customer or an existing one. This is going to take an objective perspective, so if you think it would be better to have someone else along for the ride, feel free to ask your spouse, a close friend, or even a customer of yours if they would like to help out. We tend to become subjective observers of our business, and for this exercise we want you to be able to step out of your shoes, and into the shoes of that exact customer you want to attract.

Before we can begin looking into your business with

an objective frame of mind, let's go see how other top-notch businesses handle this issue and expose ourselves to the best quality out there.

Take a couple of hours on a Saturday or Sunday afternoon, and take a trip to the local mall where the elite stores are located. Nike, Ralph Lauren, Polo, Bath & Body Works, Apple Genius Bar - any of these types of stores. Take a notepad with you so you can write down anything that strikes your fancy.

Notice their signage on the outside of the building, the colors and fonts they use for their logo, the smells as you walk in the front door, the overhead music that's playing, the way they have their displays organized, and what types of products are in those displays, the fonts they use on the header cards, the style of the carpet beneath your feet, the color of the walls, the items around the cash registers...colors and smells affect our emotions in a very big way. Once you have a good handle on your environment, look at the people who are shopping there.

What type of clothes are they wearing? What style of shoes do they have on? What about their hairstyles, age range, the color of the woman's purses, or the brand of the men's jeans? Notice the model of cars that are in the parking lot, and what colors seem to be the most popular. Anything about their customers you can identify - put it on paper. If you see something that will work great for you, write it down.

Stop by a nice art gallery, or a fine furniture store, or maybe stop into one of the upscale photography studios in your area. Make the same mental notations about what you observe there.

> *"There are plenty of great branding and marketing ideas we can find just by looking around at the world around us."*

After spending a couple of hours going in and out of several stores of this class, drive yourself over to the local department store such as Wal-Mart, K-mart, or the local 5 and dime. Make the same observations about their business as you did with the first set of businesses. What impressions do you get from looking at the outside of their building?

How do their logos and signs compare to those of the first set of businesses? When you walk in the front door, do you get the same sense of quality and value? How are the displays arranged, and how are the prices advertised? What about the people shopping there? Do they have the same style of shoes, and the same models of cars? Walk around the store a bit and get a real good sense of who it is they want to attract into their building with their branding. It won't take you long to grasp what the marketing plan is of the big discount stores. High volume, low price, load 'em up, move 'em in, move 'em out! Yee-Haw!

This exercise should also be done online as well. Spend some time studying websites of the elite brands as well as the not-so-elite ones. You will notice subtle differences that separate them all.

The Perfect Customer

What does your perfect customer look like? Is it someone who shops at a high-end boutique and pays with an AmEx card, someone who shops at the warehouse stores, or is it a combination of both? Remember that there is a difference between the type of customer you may have today, and the customer you want for tomorrow. It's all part of knowing what you want out of life, and your business.

Once this step is completed, go back to your business, and spend a few minutes reviewing the observations you just made. Now, it's on to step 2 of the process which we are going to break down into 3 categories

1) Telephone Skills Inventory

2) Physical Inventory

3) Marketing Inventory

Telephone Skills Inventory

The goal of every effective marketing campaign is, ultimately to make the phone ring, right?

"And if you can't drive the prospect to your website or to pick up the phone and call you, all the marketing in the world is useless."

Do you know how much it costs to make the phone ring, or how much is costs to drive a prospect to your website? Here's an easy way to get a fairly good idea:

If you track each call that comes into your business already, this will be easy for you. If you don't, you will need to track every call that comes in for a period, let's say a week. Of course, calls from your family, friends, and the pizza delivery shop don't count.

Then, take the total number of calls you received and divide it into your marketing total expenses for the same period. You might be surprised by the amount. I've heard of numbers as low as $3, and as high as $1,100. You can also take the number of calls and divide it into your total sales for that period, which will give you a roundabout dollar amount that each call generated. It's not an exact science, but it will give you an idea of where you are.

The first thing you want to do is to listen to your voicemail message. This ought to be fun. I bet if I did a survey of 100 businesses around the country and had them write down what they say on their answering machine, it would sound something like this….

"Hello, and thanks for calling, if you've reached this message during normal hours, we are either with a customer, on the other line, or away from the office. Please leave us your name and number and we will give you a call back when we return. Thank you - and have a nice day.

Am I close? Don't worry… it's not just people in your industry that do that… it's all of America. Do you think people get tired of listening to the same old thing every time they call a business? Why not add a little pizzazz to the mix? For example, add some funny clown music in the background, share some enthusiasm, sincerity, and some excitement in your voice. Here is a good example:

"Hi, this is BoBo the clown from BoBo's Clown School, and I'm really glad you called. If you are calling to register for clown school, press 1, if you are calling to tell me I won the lottery, press 2, if you're my wife, I'll be home for dinner by 6. If you're the taxman, you called the wrong number! Hang up and do not pass go, do not collect $200! Thanks for calling Bobo's Clown School and make it a Clowntageous DAY."

For a clown school, something over the top like that would probably fit their image well, but I'm guessing that your business will fit somewhere along the spectrum between a Clown School and a Mont Blanc pen boutique.

There are several things you should pay attention to when listening to your message. Does it sound far away and tinny? Is there the proper enthusiasm in the voice? Is it sincere? Are the words spoken clearly and concisely into the speaker, or do the words run together and sound rushed?

There is nothing worse than calling another business and having the person on the message sound bored, irritated, and disgusted, like it was a bother for them to answer the phone. It makes me not want to do business with them. You can tell the businesses you want to do business with by the way their voicemail sounds. Make your message friendly, and spirited, and welcoming. This is something you can do right now, if you so choose. Grab a piece of scratch paper, write out your script, and put a new message on your message. You can put me on pause, I'll wait.

Then we have the live person answering the phone…. (Nasally sound) (Ring, Ring) *"This is ABC Plumbing, home of the $49 septic tank extravaganza - how may I direct your call?"*

You want to sound approachable, trustworthy, professional, and glad to be alive! *"Good Morning or Good afternoon, or Good evening, or Happy Holidays, or Happy New Year! This is Mitche, how can I help you today?"* If you use your first name, you are much more likely to have them give you their first name without having to ask for it. Once you have their first name…. USE IT! People feel important and special when they hear their name, and it makes a conversation more personable. Ask questions and then shut up.

"The best way to show customers you value them is to listen, hear them out. We were given two ears and one mouth for a reason!"

Treat each call that comes into your business-like gold. That's what pays the bills, and that is what buys you the lifestyle you have chosen. If you have a staff person who handles a majority of the inbound calls, you need to make sure they fully understand that it's your image on the line each and every time they pick up the receiver to say hello. The phone is our first opportunity to make a positive impression on your marketplace, and there isn't an opportunity to make another first impression.

If your business lives completely online, then these same techniques can be used to evaluate each element of your brand that exists on someone's computer and phone when they bring up your website or social media platforms. Although you may not have a brick and mortar location, your prospects still make judgments about you in 5 seconds and will decide if they are interested in spending their hard-earned money with you......or not!

The 2nd category of the 5-Second Image Challenge is the Physical Inventory and that means taking a close look at every aspect of your business. As I mentioned earlier, it may be difficult for you to look at your business objectively, and you may want to ask someone to take this journey with you.

The thought I want you to keep in the front of your mind through this entire process is this - who is my perfect customer? Do you want to cater to old school, new school, or somewhere in-between? There's plenty of both to go around, you just need to know who your perfect customer is when trying to understand the dynamics of your brand.

PHYSICAL LOCATION

We are going to start with the outside of your entire business, whether it be retail us out of your home, so if you're located out of your home. If you have a retail location, drive down the street a couple of blocks and turn around. As you go through this process, it's important you write down everything you notice, and I suggest you create 2 columns.

One column will be for things that can be taken care of rather easily, like raking leaves or washing a window, and a 2nd column for things that may require a financial investment or a large amount of time, like painting the fence or getting new furniture.

Now, you want to put yourself in the mind of the consumer or your perfect customer. As you make your way closer, make a note of everything you see. Remember everything a potential customer observes about your business goes into what they are going to be willing to pay for your products and services.

"The higher the perceived value you have to your clients, the more you can charge, and the more referrals you get."

As you stand outside and observe your business, consider the following questions:

- Are there weeds on the side of the driveway that need to be taken out?
- What about any fence you may have?
- Is it in good shape, or could it use a couple of nails and a fresh coat of paint?
- What about the stripes that separate the parking spots?
- Are they freshly painted or are they faded from age?

- How does the paint look around the building?
- Does it look fresh and crisp, or does it remind you of the QuikMart next to the lake?
- Are the shrubs and bushes properly trimmed and groomed?
- Are your flower baskets overflowing with weeds and dead flowers?
- What about the lawn? Do you have a regular scheduled day each week when the mowing is done, and maintenance is performed?

Look at the sidewalk, or the walkway:

- Are there weeds growing up in the cracks, are their cigarette butts, and gum wrappers in visible sight?
- Are there dead leaves scattered all over the ground?
- Do you deadhead your flowers on a regular basis?
- What about the windows?
- Are there consistently washed, or can you see fingerprints and dirt on them?

Having a top-quality image means that <u>some</u> things go unnoticed. If a window is clean, you don't even notice it, do you? But you will notice if there are prints and smudges all over it. If the grass is neatly mowed, you don't notice that it doesn't need mowing. Keep an open mind as you go through this process.

Now, we are going to walk inside your business for the first time:

- Does your entrance way invite you in?
- Do you have clear and legible signs that shows your hours of operation?
- Is it professionally done, or do you use a dry erase board?
- As you walk in, how does it make you feel? Does it give you that WOW feeling?
- Does that feeling match the image you want to build?
- What smells do you notice?
- Is it fresh and clean, or old and musty?
- What part of your business do you see first?
- Does it look clean and organized?

"When people walk into one of my businesses, I want them to feel something, an emotion that evokes a positive reaction."

Above all, make sure that the feeling you get must match with your personality, style and ultimately, your personal and professional goals. I don't pretend to be the highfalutin type, with a baby grand piano and Victorian furniture spread around.

That's just not who I am, and it's not my style. We each have our own individual style, and I like mine to be a little on the countryside of life.

We each build our business, image, or marketing programs around who we are as human beings. Before they even get a sniff of what we charge for our products and services…. They know who we are and what we can do for them. Once we have them hooked on everything else, our prices become secondary.

- How do your walls look?
- Is there dust on the pictures, or cobwebs in the corner?
- What about the lighting?
- Are all the lights working, or do you have a couple that have burned out over time?
- Are the bulbs the proper wattage?
- Take notice of the carpet. Are there stains from spilled sodas, and pizza parties, and potato chips ground in?
- Does the color of your carpet match the feeling you want to evoke?
- What about your seating…… do you keep current with the latest styles and fabrics?
- Are your reading materials kept current, or

do you still have the 1999 issue of People magazine?

- Do you have books of fine art for your customers to browse, or do you have a bin full of Comic books?

Anything you have is okay, if it fits in with the image you want for your business, and what image you want to show your customers.

"Perception is a powerful motivator."

Are your shelves and counter tops wiped down on a regular basis? Do you have candles located around your business that add a sense of quality to the air? When a customer walks into your business or home for the first time, all their senses are on high alert? Sight, sound, touch, and smell. All those senses go into how they "feel".

Not everybody has top of the line designer leather furniture and turn of the century Victorian art pieces in their business, but we each need to make sure what we do have, is equal to the image we want to create, and the perfect customer we want to do business with.

Take the same steps with your public bathrooms, and hallways to and from. The image of your entire business is like one big apple pie, and everything we have talked about are vital ingredients in making the best apple pie recipe we can.

Do you have snacks available in case they want something to munch on? I know a several business owners that will take a fresh batch of chocolate chip cookies every single day and you can smell 'em as soon as you get out of the car. That makes a person feel good inside. Anything you can do to make that customer enjoy themselves even just a little bit more is worth doing. If customers enjoy themselves during their time with you, they will spend more money, and will send you more referrals.

That's it for the Physical Inventory Challenge -how did you do? You hopefully have a few pages of projects and things to do in and around the business/home over the next several weeks and months. Don't feel overwhelmed with the amount of stuff you wrote down. It just shows you have lots of potential for future growth and improvement.

To make it a bit more manageable, you can break your list up into a weekly task list. Get your staff involved, and your family, or have a neighborhood work party, and throw everyone a BBQ complete with beverages as their payment. Have some fun with it, and get other people excited about getting involved. Life is meant to be enjoyed, whether we are playing, or working.

If your storefront is virtual, meaning that your business exists 100% online, then it is even more vital that you have everything meticulously groomed with a fine-tooth comb. You must treat your website and social media platforms as if they were a brick and mortar storefront and evaluate each element in the same way you would if you had a physical location.

Marketing Inventory

Once you are done with the Physical Inventory, it's time for the 3rd category…. The Marketing Inventory. This one, you can sit down for. You will need to grab every piece of printed literature you have such as business cards, price list, brochures, information handouts, reorder forms, coupons, contracts, direct mail pieces, newspaper ads, yellow page ads, anything you hand out, mail out, or stuff into something….and of course a good cup of coffee! Put everything in a pile in front of you and go through each piece one at a time.

"Our marketing literature is a big determining factor in what position we occupy in the mind of the consumer."

The quality of the paper it's printed on, the font selection, the quality of the ink, the color of the paper stock, and the way we present it to our customers. It's all part of the apple pie. Do we just hand them a piece of paper with our prices on it, or do we package it in an elegant envelope, with gold foil lettering, finished with a gold seal? Perception, Perception, Perception.

It all depends on the industry you are in, where you want to position your business, and what lifestyle choices you have made for yourself and your family.

If you are not exactly sure how to improve on what you already have, take a look at some of your competitors literature, and at some marketing materials from other industries such as your life insurance policy, Franklin mint plate sales flyers, the welcome kit from your local Chamber of Commerce, sales flyers you get in the mail, wedding invitations you have received, the list goes on and on.

These are all things that can give you fresh ideas on how to improve your marketing literature. You can do anything you want, if you just open you mind up to new and innovative ideas from outside of the box. I challenge you to invest some time and money to create a unique look for your business that is unequalled in your market.

There are a few other quite simple ways you can enhance your image and create greater value for your products and services.... Say thank you.... Any opportunity you have to say those 2 magic words should be treasured and taken advantage of. We should all never pass on a chance to make our customers feel special and appreciated. This alone can make all the difference in the world in your business this year!

"Say thank you and mean it. Say it a lot."

Send thank you notes within 24 hours of their visit or call them to say thank you for their Internet order. I can guarantee that whatever industry you are in, hardly ANY of your competitors will be taking this extra step to assure they are taking care of their prospects or customers in that fashion.

You have other occasions to touch their lives during the year also such as special cards on their birthday, anniversary, job promotion, awards they receive, Holiday cards, or for no reason whatsoever. You will be amazed how much goodwill you can create from simple gestures like this.

"There are two kinds of service - great and bad. The mediocre makes little or no impression on most people."

Make it your goal to go above and beyond the call of duty when it comes to providing gold medal top-notch #1 rated customer service. This is the best way to create customers for life and keep the referral highway filled with traffic. Remember.... referrals are FREE.

The most difficult part of the wonderful world of branding is learning to understand the way the world around us works. The way perceptions are created, and judgments are made about you, and by you.

How value, and perceived value, is ultimately controlled by you, and how the entire process begins with the creative juices only you can provide. Your brainstorming can lead to incredible breakthroughs for your business, and your life. Without brainstorming, we wouldn't have things like ice cream cones or toilet paper!

I want to share a story about the Vice President of Marketing of a Fortune 500 company who had an innovative idea for a new product. The rest of the board had their hesitations about his idea, but he believed so firmly that he convinced them to grant him permission to proceed with the project. A few months later, when the project had completely and utterly failed, at the tune of about $3 million dollars, the VP was clearing out his office one afternoon, when the President of the company walked in.

"Where are you going?" the President asked.

"I'm clearing out all my personal things and going home. I just made a huge mistake that cost your company $3 million dollars. I assumed I was fired!" he said.

"Are you crazy?" the president said, "I just invested $3 million dollars in your education."

Every idea you come up with isn't going to be a homerun, and many will probably end up being strikeouts. There is nothing worse in this world than never even swinging the bat. Risk is part of success. Those who are willing to stick their neck out each day like you do, are the true heroes of our industry.

"You cannot experience the joy of discovering new lands, if you never risk losing sight of the shore."

Chapter 3:

Perception is Everything

Brand perception is incredibly important in business, especially when it comes the prices you choose to attach to your products and services. Do you want to be perceived as expensive and exclusive, or cheap and average? Are you perceived as a newbie in the industry or an expert? Perception holds more meaning than you can imagine, especially when it comes to pricing in your business.

I once knew a businessperson who had been in his industry for over 40 years and was known for his award-winning work. He had vast numbers of international and national awards hanging on his wall, had a past client list that included Presidents and movie stars, and was one of the best there was.

Here's the flip side of that coin....his store front looked like it was painted in the 60's (which it was!), his marketing collateral was printed using outdated fonts and cheap paper, and his business cards were kept in his back pocket so they had the infamous "butt curl".

The furniture throughout his office was dated and smelled musty, which left the air void of any fragrances that evoked positive emotions.

Business had gotten so tough for him that he had been dropping his prices over time to the point that he was barely able to cover his costs. His products were delivered to his high-end clients in cheap plastic bags that he bought at the local Dollar Tree. Needless to say, his brand was broken.

It didn't matter how great he was at what he did, the perception was that he was not a professional and his business suffered because of that perception.

Just down the street was another business in the same industry that had just opened. The owner had decided that after a 15-year career in the advertising game she would try her hand at something new.

Her store front was warm and inviting with fresh colors and modern design elements. When you walked in there was a captivating fragrance of fresh-baked cookies, her walls were filled with modern art with designer frames, and her products were delivered in elegant branded boxes with tissue paper that matched the colors of her logo. Every detail about the customer experience was painstakingly thought about and executed on.

In comparison, her prices were triple her competition, yet she seemed to always be busy. It had nothing to do with the quality of her work but had everything to do with what her perceived value was. People gladly paid a premium price for her products, and it had nothing to do with how long she had been in the industry.

Once you have decided where you want to position and brand yourself in the price market, it will be difficult to change, unless you decide to go through a re-brand. Remember, once a potential customer believes something, it is virtually impossible to change their mind.

"When a customer complains about price, you just haven't shown them enough value for the price you are asking."

You should be proud of your prices! "Yes, we are the most expensive, but let me tell you why………"

Your prices need to be based on what the market will bear, not on your expenses. If your prices are too low, it will scare people away. It's not that our clients won't pay our prices, but rather that we are afraid to charge what we are worth. This doesn't mean you need to raise your prices through the roof tomorrow, but you do need to be acutely aware of your current price position in the market and have a well-defined course of action on where you want to be in the future.

If you want to position yourself differently down the road, start making changes TODAY that will lead you down the road to success. Don't wait another day to make the necessary changes to assure a better tomorrow.

The key to good branding is you must be heard and must be noticed in a crowded marketplace. You want people to talk about you and be able to easily find you. Your goal is to first create awareness for yourself, then to create value.

Regardless of what you are selling, I guarantee there is someone else out there selling it cheaper, better, and faster. So why would they pay more for your product or business? The key is in your perceived value. They need to "think" they will get more from you than the guy down the street. If you don't already believe in yourself and your ability, why would anyone else?

It's like the often-told story of Picasso who was sitting outside one day and a woman passing by asked if he would do a quick sketch of her likeness. When he was done the lady asked, "How much do I owe you?

He said, "That will be $2000 please."

The lady said, "For 20 minutes of your time?"

He said, "No, for a lifetime of experience."

If you have something great but don't have a way of letting people know about it, you will fail.

Pricing Perception

Pricing is an interesting part of a customer's perception. If you are known to be the lowest priced business in your market, you will never be associated with high quality or great service. If you walked onto a car dealership and saw a BMW for sale for the price of a Ford Escort, you would be leery and suspicious. Something must be wrong with it to be priced that low. The opposite is also true - If a Volkswagen were for sale for the price of a Mercedes Benz, there wouldn't be many takers.

A few years ago, I had a riding lawn mower I decided to sell, and so I took an ad out in the local paper asking $50. It had seen better days, but it still ran and would cut grass just fine. I just didn't want to be bothered with the hassle of trying to sell it. A week went by and not a single call. The second week went by, nothing. By the third week, I began to realize what was taking place, and raised the price up to $200. BAM! The calls came flooding in, and I got the asking price. Priced at $50, people thought there must be something wrong with it, and so there were no takers.

What Are You Worth?

What are you worth? More importantly... what do you *want* to be worth? When you work for yourself, you have both the joy and the anguish of deciding what your products and services are worth to someone else, and to figure out ways to communicate that with potential customers. If you want to be known as the low guy on the totem pole, which I hope nobody out there does, you will never be known for offering the best quality or the best service.

"We always expect to pay more for good quality, and great service."

No questions asked. When you want to go out to a nice meal complete with soft candlelight and romantic music playing, with a gourmet wine selection and hand-carved chocolate bunnies for dessert, you will pay a premium fee. We call this selling the sizzle with the steak. When you want something quick and easy without all the glitz and glamour, you will pay substantially less.

How do people perceive your business? Are you the intimate little bistro where you would expect to spend $100 on a nice meal, or are you the drive-through where $2.95 will get you the works? More importantly, where do you want to be in the future?

There will always be plenty of business at the bottom of the pile, but it comes with an extremely high price. The old saying, "It sure is lonely at the top," but the lunches are much better.

"Customers don't pay us for the cost of our time; they pay us for the value of our time, and the value we bring to their life."

If we show up 10 minutes late for a meeting wearing flip-flops and a T-shirt, it shows the customer we don't value ourselves very much, so why should we expect them to value us? If you want to be a Cadillac, act like a Cadillac, dress like a Cadillac, and project an image like a Cadillac.

If people like you and refer others to you- that has tremendous value. It means there is a demand for your time, which means you can charge more for your products and services. Your prices need to be based on what the market will bear and what your perceived value is, not simply on your expenses.

You cannot NOT brand your business, just like you cannot NOT communicate. If someone calls you and you answer the phone, you are branding. If someone calls and you don't answer the phone, you are still branding your business. If your business card is wrinkled and stained and is in the shape of your butt, you are communicating a message.

Positioning comes down to how others view you. Branding is the way you shake hands, the way your voice sounds on the phone, how you look, how you walk, it's as much style as it is substance. The best marketing plan costs your absolutely nothing.

When you go to the store and buy something, you aren't just buying a product you are buying a perception that the product is going to fill a need that you have.

If you want to be viewed as a professional you must dress, act, and be a professional. Don't walk into an important meeting with a 50-cent pen and expect them to spend $5000 with you. Something as simple as a pen can paint a picture in your client's mind, either a positive image or a negative one. If you are the $99 Get-You-Everything guy, then a .50 cent pen will be more than enough, but if you have bigger fish to fry, you need to be aware of what is happening.

How do you create value for yourself? One of the key ways to create a higher perceived value is to under-promise and over-deliver every time in your business dealings. If you tell your customer their order will be done in four weeks, make sure they are ready in 3. If you quote someone $500 on a project, come in less. It's all part of giving them that positive experience that will reap rewards for your years to come.

I love a group called Mannheim Steamroller and their leader Chip Davis. Many of you may recognize the name, and if not, you would be familiar with their music if you heard it on the radio. You can walk into any music store year-round and find a big display of their music, and it's never on sale. What they do to motivate us to purchase is they will include a free CD of holiday music, or will send you a free BBQ sauce kit, or a large tin of gourmet hot chocolate.

I am one of those people who will always look for the unique and different, and their approach to branding is just that. With millions of album sales to their credit, I'm surprised more musicians haven't borrowed the technique. From personal experience, I can tell you the BBQ sauce goes great with chicken, and the hot chocolate is wonderful on those cold nights in front of the fire!

Here's a rule of thumb that I encourage you to make part of the fabric of your business. Don't discount.... Give stuff away... Let me say that again.... Don't discount. Give stuff away.

"When you discount- you penalize good clients and attract the price shoppers. Instead of offering some sort of discount that attract clients into your business, and diminishing the perceived value of your products, give them something for free that adds value to their purchase, or brings some joy to their lives."

The fun part for you as a High-Voltage Branding wizard, you can do anything you want, just make sure it's something they can't get from any of your competitors. That way you continue to gain ownership of your hook and category each day. Obviously, whatever you do needs to make sense financial, and only you know what your restrictions and limits are.

One thing you will find as you begin to brainstorm and come up with creative marketing and branding programs is that you will have some good ideas, and some not so good ideas, and you have to be willing to try them both.

Whether you are Bic pen in your market or the Cross pen, and there is plenty of room for both, adding value to your customer's lives should be one of the most important aspects of your branding philosophy. There is always a way to add value, whether it be real or perceived.

The most difficult part of the wonderful world of Branding is in learning to understand the way the world around us works. The way perceptions are created, and judgments are made about you, and by you. How value, and perceived value, is ultimately controlled by you, and how the entire process begins with the creative juices only you can provide. Your brainstorming can lead to incredible breakthroughs for your business, and your life.

Chapter 4:

Real vs. Perceived Value

What's the Difference?

How do you create value for yourself? As mentioned in the previous chapter, one of the key ways to create a higher perceived value is to under-promise and over deliver every time. Value is not the same as cost. Cost is what we pay to purchase something. The value of something to our customer needs to be significantly more than the selling price or they don't have an incentive to buy.

Let's say you have a product in your business that sells for $100, or should I say you want to sell for $100. Most of us can think of something in our business that sells for that price point. Through all your marketing efforts, and advertising, and promotional pieces, and positioning, and image creation, you want customers to flock to your business, whether it be physical or online, and pay $100 for let's say it's a Black Super Sonic Whatsahoosit-Plus widget. Now, whether you are successful at selling the Black Super Sonic Whatsahoosit-Plus widget is completely dependent on value or the "perceived value" it has to your client. Basically, one of three marketing phenomena is going to take place.

First, your client's perception of your widget is only $50, in which case you would have to discount by 50% to have a successful campaign. This is a popular technique before the holiday, or after the holidays for many of the chain stores. They motivate us with a very deep discount to lure us into the confines of their retail store, in the hopes you will purchase more than the item that is 50% off.

Groceries stores are famous for this technique. They will run an ad for $1.49 milk, or .29 Black Olives, or ears of corn 10 for a buck... and on your way to the farthest corner of the store to pick up your gallon of milk... you pass large end cap displays with 600 rolls of paper towels, or 1000 cans of pumpkin pie filling, or cherry cordial for .99 cents, and you can rest assured those items carry with them a nice profit margin.

The stores know intimately through their marketing research that for every 10 gallons of milk they sell at $1.49, they will also sell a fair number of other products as well. They make up for their discount on milk with sales from other high profit items. This technique is called using a "loss-leader" to attract customers in the door that can easily be adapted to a smaller business.

In the professional photography industry it's most prevalent in the Senior Market, where sessions are offered at pennies on the dollar, or for free to attract the seniors into the studio, then the volume is made up with sales from their packages and wall portraits. If you have strong sales program and effective salespeople to work with, this can be an effective strategy.

Second, the customer's perception of your widget is right at $100. Not more, not less. Right at $100. This is strategically worked to perfection by companies like Starbuck's, Apple, and Tesla. They create a demand for their products in such a way that we will gladly pay the asking price, just so we can be associated with that product. It's more about our image and making us feel special than it is what price we pay. They have made us believe that the price really isn't that important. We want to belong to the "club" so to speak.

When you go to buy a Tesla, the asking price is also the selling price… No dickering, no negotiating. If you want to drive a Tesla and belong to their "brand", this is the price. If you are a 'Buckhead", someone who gets their coffee at Starbuck's, the same dynamic is at play.

Third… You manage to create a "perceived value" in the mind of the customer some point more than $100.

Maybe it's $120, maybe $150, maybe $200 or more. The greater the discrepancy between the selling price and the perceived value, the higher the level of motivation your customer will have, and the greater the level of sales you will have. This is done primarily by adding additional value to their purchase. The sky really is the limit here, and the more creative you get, the better your response will be. Remember one of the basic rules of marketing...

"Either you are different and unique, or you are out of business. Find out what everyone else is doing, then don't do it. Run as fast as you can in the other direction!"

This is how you guarantee you will separate yourself from the rest of the pack.

Look at the infomercials on TV. They will spend the first 25 minutes of the show creating a value in our minds of $19.95.... And most of the time, we probably believe that's what the product is worth. Then suddenly, they sweeten the pot and say, "If you call in the next 7 minutes, we will include a second one absolutely free." You see it time and time again, so it obviously works, or they wouldn't continue doing it.

If the value in the mind of the customer is greater than the asking price, BOOM.... You have a good chance of making the sale. The bottom line in all this is simple...

Always give your customers value that is greater than the price they pay.

That's the question of the day... How can we create a value in our products (perceived or real), that motivates people to want to do business with us? Perceived Value is strongly influenced by emotion, ego, personal image, things that are intangible and should all be considered in your marketing programs.

One thing you will find as you begin to brainstorm and come up with creative marketing programs is that you will have some good ideas, and some not so good ideas, and you have to be willing to try them both. An idea I tried a few years ago for my wedding business sounded great at the beginning but turned out to be a lot of work in the end, and I'm sure you'll see why after I tell you this story.

Back in the 1990's I had photography studios and was looking for an innovative idea that I could use to entice and motivate potential wedding clients to book my studio instead of my competitors. So, I went out and purchased a professional limousine company, complete with a chauffeur and website. Originally, I was going to use it for people who signed a contract at a Bridal Fair, but I ended up using it the entire year.

My idea was this: for every 1 hour of coverage, you had in your wedding collection, I would provide one hour of limousine rental for free.

For example, if the client had a 5-hour wedding package, they would get a nice limousine for 5 hours, and it didn't have to be at the same time. That way they could use it to pick up the wedding party from home, or shuttle guests from the church to the reception, or whatever they chose. Well, instead of working some sort of arrangement with a local company, I decided to just go out and purchase the entire company…. Lock, stock, and barrel.

The idea was a tremendous success. Our booking rate went through the roof, and we became the "talk of the town." Our clients absolutely loved what we did for them, but I had just purchased a business, complete with a toll-free number and a yellow page ad! The calls came in at all hours from 8am Sunday morning to 11pm Tuesday night for weddings, birthday parties, anniversaries, business get-togethers, sweet-16 parties. It was a real business, which meant I had to arrange coverage 24/7, for the phone and for a driver.

Many times, I ended up being the chauffeur, the mechanic, and the person who washed the limo. It did very well as a business, but it became very time-consuming and took the focus away from what the original intention was which was to provide my clients with something unique and different that would position my studio in their minds as a cut above the competition. After about 1 year, I decided to sell the company and move on to other ideas.

Regardless of the outcome of your ideas, you must be willing to risk failure to attain the highest level of success.

"Be bold, be adventurous, and have some fun!"

As you can see, creating value for yourself and your company takes on many different faces and comes in a vast plethora of colors. It's all up to you and what your goals are in life. It's amazingly easy for us to fall into that old management trap and get caught-up in the day-to-day details of running our business. We end up running of our businesses instead of designing our lives. We all fall prey to it from the day-to-day stuff such answering phones, meeting with prospects and customers, ordering supplies, mowing the lawn, etc. Before we know it, our free time is gone, and there is no time for the things in life that are profoundly important, like family and personal hobbies.

For example, you might be working Friday nights, Sunday mornings, and holidays. You don't have time to play with your children or take a drive with your family along the lake or read that good book you've been meaning to get to or practice your putting at the golf course. The things that are most important to us start slowly slipping away and we become a slave to our business rather than its master.

Whether you are the top of your market or somewhere in the middle, and there is plenty of room for both, adding value to your customer's lives should be one of the most important aspects of your branding philosophy. There is always a way to add value. Not everyone can be the Cadillac, in fact there's only 1, and not everyone wants to buy a Cadillac. Some people want to buy a Lexus, or a Tesla, or a minivan, or a Ford Escort, or a Mustang.

It's okay to borrow other ideas from within your industry, and outside of your industry. You don't need to reinvent the wheel. Just find an idea that already exists and customize it to meet your personality and style.

"Since you can't be all things to all people, find what you are good at, and make it your trademark- your personal stamp."

The day of Jack-of-all-Trades is long gone, and the age of specialization is upon us. Whatever position or niche you want to occupy in the customer's mind, everything you do should be with that in mind, and be consistent with your goals and objectives.

We have the honor and the privilege to not only sell fine products and services to our customers, but to sell ourselves as well. Believing in yourself and your abilities as a branding powerhouse can bring you rewards too great to number. The challenge of creating effective branding programs that position yourself in exactly the place you want to be, can be difficult at times, but also one of the most fulfilling and rewarding feelings you will ever have, but you have to be willing to run away from the rest of the crowd.

Separating yourself from the rest of the pack is never easy, but can take you to places never dreamed of, if you are willing to take the risk.

Life is NOT a spectator, sport.

Chapter 5:

Personal Branding

To many people, their personal brand (PB) is what makes them successful in their chosen field. You may be one of them. Your entire business model is built on you as a person, your personality, your trust factor, your essence. If you look at some of the top brands in the world, you will notice that at the forefront of their brands is an individual- someone who encapsulates the very essence of what the company stands for. I'm going to give you a short quiz and I want you to envision the brand in your mind.

Microsoft

Amazon

Facebook

Tesla

When you saw the name of the business, what was the first thing that popped into your brain? Was it a logo, or was it a person? Did you see Bill Gates, Jeff Bezos, Mark Zuckerberg, and Elon Musk before you thought about any logo? This is the power of PB, and your reputation and image are probably intimately tied to the brand of your business.

Self-branding can help increase your reputation as a leader, position yourself as the expert in your industry or become an influencer within your niche. You can build a personal brand that resonates with people all over the world by having an active presence in person and online and showcasing your business, talents, or skills.

It's more about creating a brand around YOU as a person, rather than strictly the business. In other words, PB can further your career by positioning yourself as the expert in your field, grow your social following that could lead to a better job, increase your opportunities and sell more products or services in your business. Online educators, authors, personal YouTube channels, celebrities and sports stars all have personal brands that create value for their "empires".

It doesn't happen overnight because it takes some planning and hard work to see results. In the process, you may discover that you have room for improvement after receiving feedback from others.

One way to get started is to create a personal branding statement that clearly defines your audience and what you can offer them. Place this statement in a visible place in your office, on your computer, and on your phone to remind yourself to stay true to that statement.

Credibility

People buy from people they know, like and trust...plain and simple. PB gives you more credibility and is so important in this day and age when more people are looking for people and brands they can put their trust in.

To get noticed, you need to put yourself out there! It's about creating a portfolio about YOU. As a result, more people will get to know you, realize the value you bring to the table, and can lead to more referrals in whatever your industry is.

New Opportunities

PB can also help you get new opportunities, marketing partnerships, and business deals that you would not otherwise hear or know about. Branding yourself instills credibility and trust in your abilities and knowledge and allows you to show your personality that differentiates you from others in your field. Aligning with your personal branding statement will help you continue and make progress with your goals.

Steps to create your personal brand:

1) Create your PB statement.

2) Define your perfect customer.

3) Plan to engage with your target audience and promote positive participation with them. (Chamber Greeters, Rotary Club, Kiwanis, networking groups, online Facebook groups, etc.)

4) Commit to sharing your personal brand through networking, speaking engagements, and social media.

5) Celebrate the small and big wins as this will keep you motivated!

How can you tell if you are being successful at your personal branding efforts?

- You get asked to speak at a conference or event.

- Someone else refers you to a potential customer or client

- A publication (online or in print) asks you to write an article or blog

- You get the sale or project

- People mention you on social media, their blog or online

Be Patient

Personal branding is time-consuming and frankly, never ends! Slacking off is never good and you must keep in tune with your industry. Take the time to delve deeper into your industry and ask the hard questions that will help you remain true to yourself and your personal/professional goals.

Consistency is the Key

Self-branding requires you to be consistent in your work, beliefs, and recognize that your followers identify with you, often in more ways than one. If you change any of the above, they will not trust you or your personal brand in the future. And it is not just about making posts on social media every single day. It is also about unifying your message with the same look when it comes to personal branding. Give your audience and customers what they fell in love with in the first place.

Be Authentic

What makes you original? What are your special traits? Are you quirky about something – perhaps how you present yourself to the world? What makes you stand out? Personal branding is about celebrating your differences and requires you to be authentic as you let your true self shine.

Become a Blogger

If you are consistent in creating content, you will be amazed at how blogging can create and build an audience around you and your business. You can start out by offering to create a blog in your industry publications or build your own blog. Using blogging for your personal branding is an excellent way to build an audience around you and it allows you to create online value for your business.

Give Value to Your Audience

Give, give, give....and give some more! Whatever service or business you are in, it is important to give value to your audience and customers. That could include informative articles about specific products or services, tip of the day, or tutorial videos. Your customers could certainly buy from a company that simply runs endless ads, but by giving value to your audience, you will gain their loyalty because you taught them something of value. Give, give, give....and give some more!

Network

You must put yourself in front of the buying public

and that means mingling with people at social events or conferences, joining a meet-up event, posting on social media consistently, and interacting with people as much as possible. This is what networking is all about and allows you to expand into other areas or categories that you may have never thought about. You may meet someone who can help or has experience in an area that you would like to expand on in the future. You never know where networking will lead!

Be Creative

While I know it is important to be consistent with your message, you can certainly be creative when it comes to social media such as Facebook or Instagram. Showing your "personal" side may help build your credibility as a professional. You will be amazed how much it can strengthen your personal branding efforts.

Position Yourself as the Expert

What is your niche? Do you sell product online? Build your personal brand around your expertise. For example, if you are in the fitness industry, build your brand around your specialty in that arena. Write articles, help people lose weight and encourage them to share their experience with you.

Interact with your Followers

Your personal brand cannot be built without interacting with people, especially your followers. Take time each day to respond to their messages. If someone tagged you in their post, acknowledge it and thank that person. If you wrote an article and discovered it was shared on social media, thank them for doing that. If one of your followers has a question about you or your business, take the time to answer their question. All the above will help cultivate and personalize you and your personal brand.

Chapter 6:

Developing a "Blue Ocean" Strategy

When it comes to branding your business, you have 2 choices. Have a business that offers the same products, the same services, the same everything as all your competitors. OR you can figure out a way to develop a niche where there is little or no competition. This is called finding some blue ocean somewhere in the world.

You may already be aware of the terms 'red ocean' and 'blue ocean,' which were coined by professors Chan Kim and Renee Mauborgne through their international best-seller book "Blue Ocean Strategy".

Basically, a market that is full of competitors is known as the red ocean because all that competition turns the ocean a blood red. If you are already a business owner in today's business world, you may have been trying to figure out what you can do to blast the competition. However, do you really want to operate in that highly competitive red ocean, or would you rather figure out a way to be a pioneer in an ever-expanding blue ocean?

The hard part is dealing with all the copycats that come out of the woodwork and take advantage of the many mistakes you have made, your ideas and strategies. In other words, they can force you back into the red ocean, especially in this high-tech Internet world we live in. What can you do when you are in blue water when it is slowly turning red? It is possible to stay in the blue water and grow a profitable business, but first let's look at the differences between the red and blue ocean:

- In a red ocean, the competition already exists whereas in a blue ocean, you can create an unchallenged market space.

- The strategy in a red ocean is to beat the competition whereas in the blue water, you make the competition irrelevant.

- The competition may have an advantage in the red ocean, but the blue ocean requires innovation and value.

- The red ocean has existing customers, but the blue ocean attracts non-customers.

- Existing demand is exploited in the red ocean whereas in the blue ocean, new demand is created.

Surviving in a Red Ocean

Entrepreneurs and business leaders are constantly creating competitive strategies in a red ocean. They go head-to-head with their competition day-in and day-out over the same consumer markets. All of them are doing the exact same thing but trying to compete on price. You will never win that battle, that I know for sure.

Let's look at fast-food chains such as McDonalds, Burger King, Arby's, Wendy's, Taco Bell. To survive, they have had to offer more items, install faster ordering systems, and cater to those interested in eating healthier meals. I can't remember the last time I saw a fast-food chain that didn't have a "$1 Value Menu" displayed prominently on premises. The increased competition turns the water red fighting for more profit and growth, meaning the pressure to lower prices becomes immense.

Ways to Create a Blue Ocean

In a blue ocean, demand for services and business is created rather than waging war against your competition. There is plenty of opportunity for growth that is swift and profitable. Blue oceans can be created in two ways:

1) A company or business creates a brand-new industry – for example when Netflix first came out, nobody really had heard of watching a

movie or a show on demand streaming on the Internet. We used to have to wait a year to watch *"The Grinch"* or *"It's A Wonderful Life"* on TV or watch a rerun of *"Friends"*. Now, at the touch of a button we can watch just about every show ever created. If you have noticed, Netflix now has a RED OCEAN of competition... So, what did Netflix do a few years back? They began creating original content which kept them a step ahead of the competition. They "created" blue waters once again. Google, Apple, and Disney among others have jumped into the crowded space in the last little bit of time, and as this book is written, that blue ocean is once again turning red. I'm sure someone will come up with an innovation to the industry that will make the competition irrelevant for a short period of time, then the cycle will begin all over again!

2) Create a blue ocean within a red ocean – this can occur when a company changes the limitations of an existing industry. A good example of this occurred in the saturated fitness industry with a company called Curves. Started over 25 years ago, Curves changed fitness for women by offering studio fitness workouts at a low price. The workouts last for 30 minutes and

you have a coach during each session, as well as the support members needed to achieve their health and fitness goals. At the time, nobody else was offering a product or service that competed.

A few tips for finding and staying in the Blue Water:

- In order to find and stay in the blue water, you have to offer benefits that your competitors consider unnecessary or are overly unique. It might be something that contributes to a cleaner environment, offers a unique purpose, or a style that is distinctive, exclusive, rare, or irreplaceable.

- Create a total solution for buyers who are purchasing a product or service. A good way to do this is to consider what goes on before, during and after a product or service has been completed.

- Create a new allure or interest in an existing product.

- Search for other segments or buyer groups for your product or service.

- Approach your business from a different perspective in time – it is not about preempting or predicting trends in an industry.

- Instead of focusing on customer differences, focus on prevailing unities in what customers value.

- Focus on trying to increase the size of your industry or business by attracting people who have never purchased anything in that industry before.

- Create a high value at a low cost – a good example of this is Southwest Airlines and JetBlue who appealed to people who were used to driving to their destinations, rather than flying. In other words, they made flying affordable. Strip away any unnecessary costs – anything that doesn't contribute or create value gets reduced or eliminated. Plus, it is an efficient way to run a business regardless of what color ocean you are in.

As you can see, the concept of a red and blue ocean is much easier to understand if you look at real-world examples that exist today of how businesses have branded themselves, then rebranded themselves.

Most industries are operating in a red ocean with defined competitors, with specific ways to run their business in a defined market. It is best described as shark-infested water where all the sharks are fighting for the same prey.

You must take some time to evaluate whether you need to rethink your business strategies and branding to create a blue ocean for your products and services. This is fun and challenging at the same time!

If you are spending all your time fighting for a piece of limited sales, then you are in a red ocean and you need to stop, right now! You are probably constantly competing with your competitors just to increase your market share as your business becomes more competitive and aggressive with more and more competitors coming in. Profits are likely to diminish as well, and eventually you will go out of business.

When companies compete for the same customers with the same products, same features, same benefits, the result is a pricing war and you will ALWAYS end up a loser in the scenario.

Just remember that once you are successful in the blue water, other companies will be attracted to you and quickly change your blue water space to red. When this occurs, and I bet my bottom dollar that it will, you must differentiate yourself. Saying that you are 'the original' only works for so long before it doesn't matter anymore. You may be forced to customize your product more or offer other services to keep yourself in the blue water, but it will be totally worth it.

Chapter 7:

Delivering a "6-Star Experience"

As the digital revolution continues to take root in our cultures, so too has the decrease in the importance of having actual humans at the front lines of a business. The Internet has taken away much of the human interaction that just a few short years ago was vitally important to business survival.

Getting gas, shopping for groceries, buying a movie ticket, getting a hot dog at a baseball game, or simply stopping at the bank to make a deposit. In my life, these are all touch points when I have the opportunity for conversation with a frontline employee during my purchase.

If I'm not greeted with at least a short and friendly *"hello, how are you today"*, or a moment of eye contact, I have no problem saying *"Hello, don't forget to greet your customers"* or *"Don't forget to smile at your customers!"* It's not that I expect to have a real conversation but do expect to at least be shown a little consideration since I'm the one paying their wage!

It drives my wife and kids crazy when I do it, but it's something I feel strongly about. To most retail-type businesses, they must depend on having those frontline folks represent their brand at the highest levels, but for some unknown reason that skill has not been given the importance that it once had. It is becoming a dying art.

If you are even a little like me, you feel the same way. We expect to have a basic level of customer service when we have some sort of interaction with a business. Get it right and they continue to get our support. Blow it and we will be happy to tell our friends and family about our bad experience.

When you hear about the accolades of the best hotels and restaurants around the world, you typically hear about the "5-Star" ratings that they have. To them, and to the customers they serve, that means they are the absolute best at what they do. There's no better number than to be given 5 stars.

I think there needs to be a new level of customer service, a new scale on how our customers judge us by. I suggest we add one more star to the scale for our businesses.

Here's an example...Right now where you are sitting, I want you to reach your arms and hands as far towards the heavens as you can. Reach, reach, reach! Have you reached as far as you can? Now, I want you to reach a little bit further.

I bet you found a little more umph inside of you to reach just a bit more, didn't you?

Why is that? You reached as far as you could the first time, but then you reached a little farther when asked.

"What does it hurt for us to give just a little bit more when it comes to providing impeccable customer service to our customer? "

I recently had my car into the body shop to repair a small dent in the front fender. When I dropped the car of along with the keys, I inadvertently forgot to take off the master key to my office. By the time I figured this out, it was the end of the day and I couldn't leave the building unlocked to go back to the body shop to get my master key.

My solution was to have a taxi go to the shop to pick up the key, then bring it to me. When I called the body shop to let them know about the plan, they GM said he would take care of making the arrangements.

About 20 minutes later the GM himself walked into my office with the key! He drove all the way across town to fix a problem that I created, not him.

That level of service was not asked for nor expected,

but it made me a customer for life with the company! Something not expected can often bring the biggest results. What can you do in your business that shows your customers that you care "just a little bit" more?

Back in the 70's there was a band called Dr. Hook, and they cranked out some of the best love songs that this world has ever seen. One of their song's muses "when you think I've loved you all I can, I'm gonna love you a little bit more".

Having a 6-Star mentality will not only revolutionize the way your business operates but will also give you a competitive edge in the market.

What does it hurt to give just a little extra?

Chapter 8

How To Build A Cult Brand

Water. It's everywhere and it's free.

This is a product that has always amazed me...something that we have access to for FREE, yet we gladly will pay good money for the convenience of not having to get it from our tap at home, or because we simply want to belong to the "brand".

In lakes, in the mountains, in our schools, in the showers, in our sinks. Remind me again WHY there are so many H2O brands on the shelves today when it's something we can get for free in most places?

We will spend anywhere between $1 and $10 on a single bottle of water not just to get hydrated, but to belong to a brand, or cult if you will. People that walk around with a bottle of Perrier don't do so because they are thirsty, they do it because they belong to a tribe, a group of like-minded people from all around the world that have bought into the Perrier brand. Dasani, Aquafina, Evian, Earth20 and more all have created cult-like followings for their brands.

We purchase over 50,000,000,000 (billion with a B!) bottles of water each year in the US alone. Worldwide that number is more than 200,000,000,000 bottles a year.

I have a secret to tell you that I'm sure most people already know, but we won't admit it to ourselves. In its purest form, water is water. There is no such thing as a "better quality" water. Assuming that it is void of any minerals or impurities and has been filtered properly, water is water. Now that we have that worked out, let's move on.

Two bottles. The same H2O inside. Two diametrically opposite markets. One is the low-end where that small bottle of water goes for pennies. The other is the high-end landscape where it goes for as much as ten bucks apiece (remember that water similar to this is available from your sink or garden house in your back yard!).

One is $1 and the other is $10. How do you pull something like that off?

Obviously through high-voltage branding where you'll first identify the "discontent" point in the high-end market; for example, "spotting a trend" (after creating a buzz!) where your targeted demographic is uncertain about what type of a glass container would be the only acceptable way to store water in its pure state. Or, perhaps, it's the source of the water that triggers the right emotion? Maybe the deep, underground reservoir containing prehistoric water would be far more marketable than just another ground-level spring or river regardless of how pure, pristine, and intact it may be in reality?

Remember, they don't know it until we tell them. They are simply open to suggestions – at all times.

Today's consumerism leaves no one immune to a well-targeted and well-crafted message. And that's the spot we are hitting with our prehistoric, deep underground reservoir from which we are pumping the water in its purest possible state and then store it in the high-quality glass bottles crafted in one of the world's most exclusive glass factories famous for casting glass for kings and queens.

Such an operation sounds quite expensive, doesn't it? Well, not necessarily.

Terms "deep" and "underground" are, of course, relative. Therefore, we will simply avoid mentioning the fact that we are extracting water from the five-foot deep basin.

Is it underground? Yes.

Is it deep? Sure. There is no way to say how deep that goes just by looking at images and videos that are online.

If we craft a compelling story and message, people

will have an emotional reaction to it. It's a basic human behavior. We want to believe. And once people are indoctrinated into our story, they will ruthlessly defend our brand at all costs.

It's not just a bottle of water. It's a statement. An ID card that our friends immediately recognize. A single, swift look and people know that we belong. It doesn't matter that we paid 1000% over the real market value, bought access. We bought a privilege.

Need I remind you that this is for something that most people in the world can get for free, with a little effort! These brands have created a sense of tribalism for their products, and with it has come tremendous profits.

"Your goal should be to create the same type of zest and zeal for your brand so that people will proclaim your name from the highest mountain top!"

A cult following for your products and services. Do this, and the rest is a piece of cake!

Nike, Apple, Harley Davidson, Gucci……need I say more?

Chapter 9

Is My Brand Broke?

The question that I hope is now floating around in that big, wonderful brain of yours is this...could my brand use an update? Do I need to consider a complete overhaul to my brand? Is my brand broke?

For many of you, these types of thoughts have never entered your mind before and I encourage you to sit down with that proverbial good cup of coffee and really give this topic some serious thought.

Maybe you are burned out and feel like throwing in the towel. Maybe you feel deep down that you are not meant for the entrepreneurial game. If it was easy, everyone would be jumping in the game with both feet.... but it's not. It's meant for a small handful of incredibly special individuals who have visions for a better world, a passion to makes lives more fulfilling. YOU are one of the chosen few!

Whether you are a conglomerate with 1000's of employees or have an enterprise with 1 employee (you!), keeping the edge of your business sword sharp is one of ls most important responsibilities you have. As time goes by, our edge can become dulled because of a variety of reasons; apathy, burnout, thinking you are too busy, business growth, or plain ole laziness.

That's ok, there's no better time than right now to put aside all your excuses and to dedicate some precious bandwidth to this topic. This book has detailed some of the steps you can take to answer these questions and has hopefully given you the motivation to take the branding bull by the horns.

Regardless of what your answers are, this can be one of the most exciting times in the history of your business. If you are still contemplating jumping into the entrepreneurial game, this is your opportunity to put some muscle behind your brand before it's even launches to the world! It's never easy to take the road less travelled, and to go above and beyond to make sure that you are keeping the edge of your sword sharp.

Once upon a time, a big, strong woodcutter got a job working for a local business. The pay was great and so were the benefits. The woodcutter was excited and determined to do his absolute best to impress the boss. His boss gave him an axe and showed him the area where he was to work.

On the first day, the woodcutter brought back

twenty-five trees. "That's great," said the boss. "Keep up the good work!" Totally motivated by his boss's encouragement, the woodcutter tried even harder the second day, but he could only bring back fifteen trees. On the third day, he only brought back ten trees. Day after day, he kept bringing back fewer and fewer.

"Something's wrong with me," the woodcutter surmised. "I'm losing my strength." He went to the boss and apologized, saying he could not understand what was going on.

"When was the last time you sharpened your axe?" asked the boss.

"Sharpened my axe? I don't have time; I've been too busy cutting down trees".

This book is about helping you get and keep your edge sharp. It's extremely easy to get caught up in the "cutting down of trees" that we forget to continue to sharpen our axe so that the business forest is easier to navigate.

> *"To get the most out of life, we must continue to be students."*

It's not about just setting goals for your business. Sharpening your focus means digging deeper to gain a clearer understanding of what you really want out of life, what your true priorities are, and how to go about reaching those goals. Whatever your business brand looks like, remember to stay true to yourself and your dreams.

As I have written in other books, finding the perfect work/life balance is something we all need to focus on every day. Life is short, life is precious, and life is sometimes fleeting.

We need to make sure that we are aware of those special "moments" that present themselves to us and take advantage of opportunities to tell the people who mean the most that we love them!

Yes, your business and your job are important aspects of your life, because you need the income they bring so you can buy the perfect lifestyle for you and your family.

But, when your time on this earth is over, all that will be remembered is the difference you made to those that meant the most to you.

Love your family, love your friends, and the rest will work itself out...

Live with Passion!

The 4X Formula-
Getting Twice As Much Done In ½ The Time
(limited spots available)

This course will be launching within the next few weeks, and now you have the opportunity to be part of the inaugural beta "A-Team", who will get some special bonuses that are available only for this group.

BONUS #1-

You'll be given lifetime access to all of the content, including any updates or additions that are made in the future.

BONUS #2-

You also will be given access to a private Facebook group where other students in the course can go to share your struggles, share your wins, and get access to Mitche to discuss the course as it develops.

BONUS #3-

You will also have exclusive access to a monthly live group video call where Mitche answers your questions, helps you with any challenges you are having, and helps facilitate the communications between group members.

And as a special bonus...

BONUS #4-

We will also send you a digital copy of the book "The Unleashed Entrepreneur – A Kick-Ass Guide To Harnessing Your Inner Ninja, Working Less, & Designing Your Perfect Lifestyle" as my gift to you.

The bonuses alone are valued at over $500, and the course will be selling for $250 once we launch this to the rest of the world.

That's A Total Value Of Over $750!

But you don't need to pay anywhere near that.

Right now, you can grab the course and the other bonuses for only $100, or 2 payments of $60 each.

ENROLL NOW
at
www.4xcourse.com

A SPECIAL THANK YOU NOTE

I deeply appreciate you taking the time to invest in your quality of life, your business, and your future! If you find the book to be beneficial, I would be grateful if you would leave an honest review on Amazon. It would mean the world to me!

Looking for more inspiration and actionable tools to grow your business and design your perfect lifestyle? Then subscribe to the hottest new show the **"Business Edge Radio"** with Mitche Graf on iTunes, Stitcher, Google Play, Spotify, or on your local talk radio station. Hear dynamic interviews with world-class entrepreneurs as well as regular dose of meat-and-potatoes techniques that will ignite your superpowers to achieve even greater things!

Additional resources can be found at www.MitcheGraf.com.

Thank you for spending this time with me, and good luck with your new set of eyes!

Mitche

www.ingramcontent.com/pod-product-compliance
Lightning Source LLC
Chambersburg PA
CBHW061748020426
42331CB00006B/1398